What Is the ELECTORAL COLLEGE?

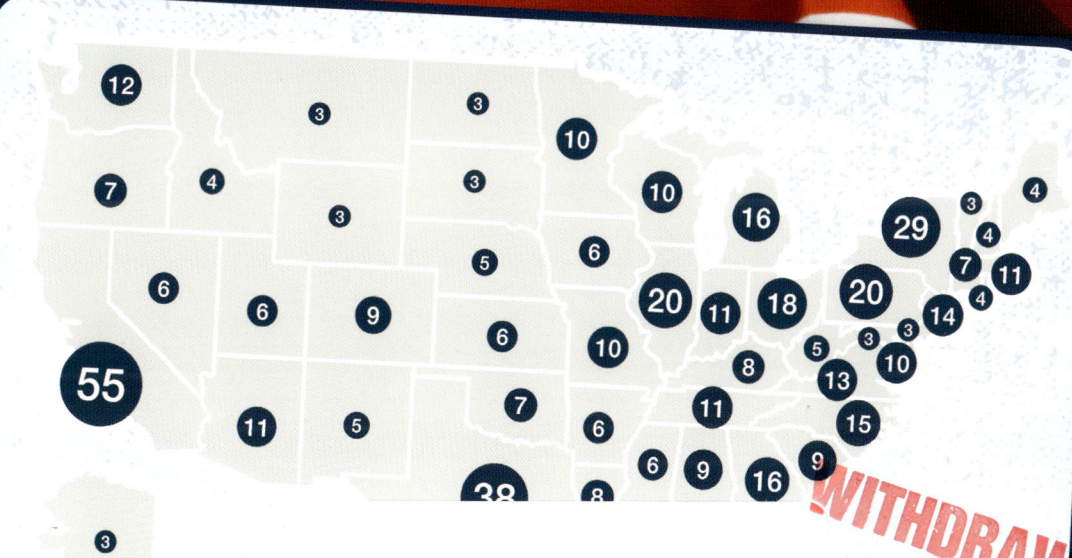

Fitchburg Public Library
5530 Lacy Road
Fitchburg, WI 53711

By Therese M. Shea

Gareth Stevens
PUBLISHING

Please visit our website, www.garethstevens.com. For a free color catalog of all our high-quality books, call toll free 1-800-542-2595 or fax 1-877-542-2596.

Library of Congress Cataloging-in-Publication Data

Names: Shea, Therese, author.
Title: What is the Electoral College? / Therese M. Shea.
Description: New York : Gareth Stevens Publishing, 2022. | Series: U.S. government Q & A! | Includes index.
Identifiers: LCCN 2020033535 (print) | LCCN 2020033536 (ebook) | ISBN 9781538264317 (library binding) | ISBN 9781538264294 (paperback) | ISBN 9781538264300 (set) | ISBN 9781538264324 (ebook)
Subjects: LCSH: Electoral college–United States–Juvenile literature. | Presidents–United States–Election–Juvenile literature.
Classification: LCC JK529 .S54 2022 (print) | LCC JK529 (ebook) | DDC 324.6/3–dc23
LC record available at https://lccn.loc.gov/2020033535
LC ebook record available at https://lccn.loc.gov/2020033536

First Edition

Published in 2022 by
Gareth Stevens Publishing
29 E. 21st Street
New York, NY 10010

Copyright © 2022 Gareth Stevens Publishing

Designer: Andrea Davison-Bartolotta
Editor: Charlie Light

Photo credits: Cover (main) 24K-Production/Shutterstock.com; cover (inset) Dimitrios Karamitros/Shutterstock.com; series art (paper, feather) Incomible/Shutterstock.com; series art (blue banner, red banner, stars) pingbat/Shutterstock.com; p. 4 Trevor Bexon/Shutterstock.com; p. 5 (left) Nuno21/Shutterstock.com; p. 5 (right) archna nautiyal/Shutterstock.com; p. 6 FrameAngel/Shutterstock.com; p. 7 Bettmann/Getty Images; pp. 7 (pins), 11 (pins) Alexander Limbach/Shutterstock.com; p. 9 (background) Iris_Images/Shutterstock.com; pp. 9 (map), 13 (states) YummyBuum/Shutterstock.com; p. 10 Sunward Art/Shutterstock.com; p. 11 (left) courtesy of Library of Congress; p. 11 (right) Everett Collection/Shutterstock.com; p. 13 (main) Rhona Wise/AFP/Getty Images; p. 15 (main) Alex Wong/Getty Images; p. 15 (inset) Wikimedia Commons/File:Certificate of Vote.png; p. 17 (main) Joe Amon/The Denver Post/Getty Images; p. 17 (inset) Paul J. Richards/AFP/Getty Images; p. 19 DNetromphotos/Shutterstock.com; p. 21 (main) Mark Makela/Getty Images; p. 21 (inset) Sarah Rice/Getty Images.

All rights reserved. No part of this book may be reproduced in any form without permission in writing from the publisher, except by a reviewer.

Printed in the United States of America

Some of the images in this book illustrate individuals who are models. The depictions do not imply actual situations or events.

CPSIA compliance information: Batch #CSGS22: For further information contact Gareth Stevens, New York, New York at 1-800-542-2595.

Contents

What Is the Electoral College?........................4
Clues in the Constitution 6
How Many Electors?...............................8
The Early Electoral College 10
Electing the Electors..............................12
Casting and Counting the Votes 14
How They Vote...................................16
Popular Vote vs. Electoral Vote 18
The Future of the Electoral College 20
Glossary..22
For More Information.............................23
Index 24

Words in the glossary appear in **bold** type the first time they are used in the text.

What Is the Electoral College?

When you think of a college, you likely think of a place for older students to study. A college can also be a group of people who have a similar job or goal.

In the United States, the Electoral College is a group of voters who elect the U.S president and vice president. Members of this group are called electors. In this book, you'll learn what happens during each step of the important election **process** the Electoral College follows.

A presidential election happens every four years in the United States. In 2020, Joe Biden and Senator Kamala Harris won the electoral vote to become U.S. president and vice president.

Clues in the Constitution

Every other government election in the United States is won through a **popular vote**. Why doesn't our **democracy** elect the president and the vice president this way?

When the U.S. Constitution was written, no country had a direct election for a president-like official. The Founding Fathers didn't think every U.S. citizen would be educated enough to vote. They also didn't think it was a good idea for Congress to choose the president. They decided states would choose electors to vote for the president.

Government Guides

Founding Father Alexander Hamilton said the Electoral College might not be perfect, but it was "at least excellent."

Alexander Hamilton

The U.S. Constitution, the highest law in the nation, was written in 1787. It set up the federal, or national, government, including the presidential election process.

How Many Electors?

The Constitution says that states can choose their electors in any way they want. Their number of electors is equal to their number of Congress members. This is based on the number of people living in the state. So, the more populated a state, the more electors it has.

Today, the Electoral College is made up of 538 electors. That's three more electors than members of Congress. That's because Washington, DC, was given electors in 1961, in the Twenty-third **Amendment**.

Government Guides

The U.S. Constitution says an elector can't be a "senator or **representative**, or person holding an office of trust" in the U.S. government.

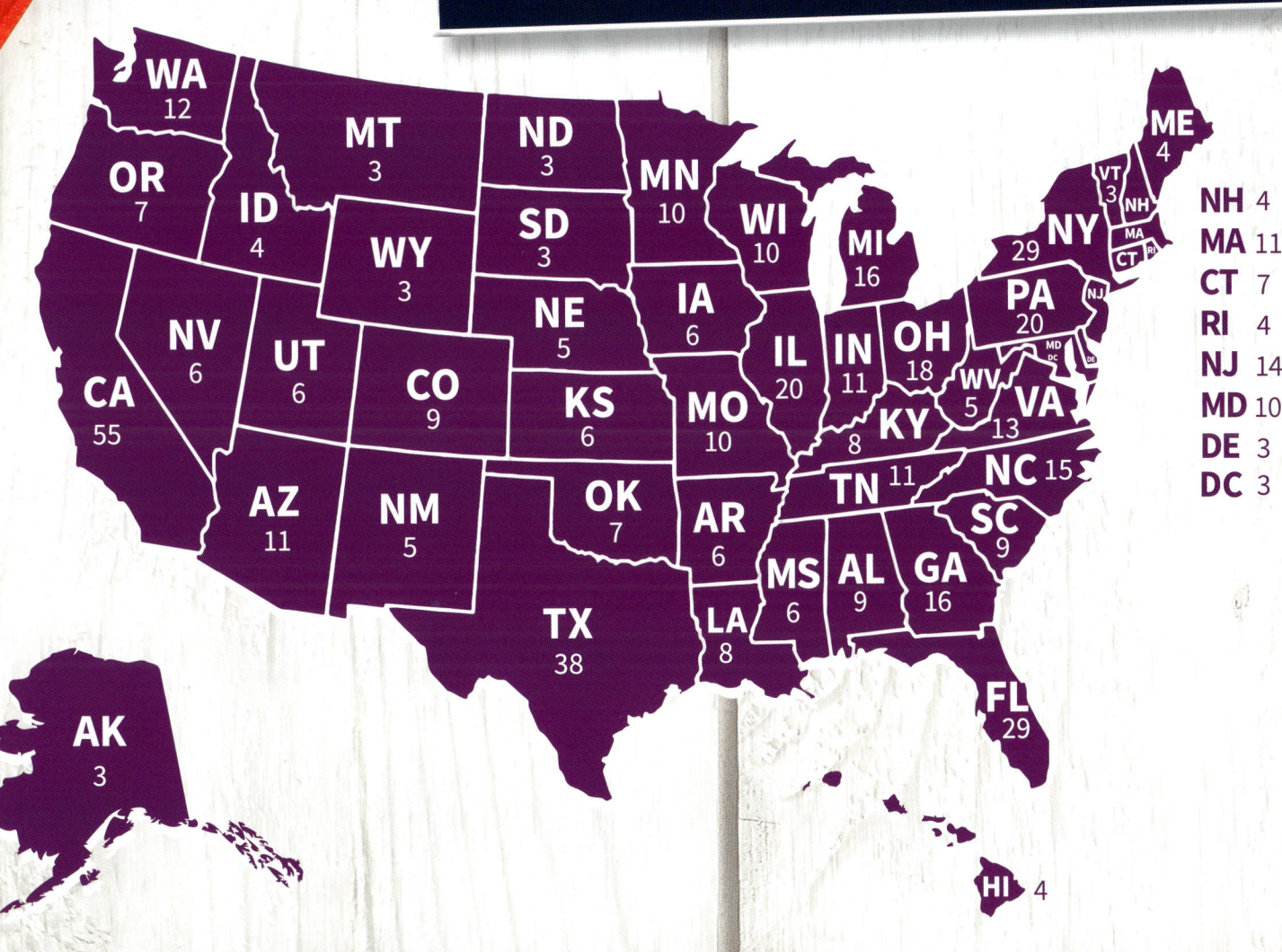

The Early Electoral College

At first, state **legislatures** were in charge of choosing electors. The **political party** with the most members in the state legislature picked the electors. These electors were expected to vote for the candidates belonging to that political party.

Each elector was allowed two votes for president. The candidate with the most votes won the presidency. The candidate in second place became the vice president. Today, each elector votes for a president and a vice president separately.

◀ Aaron Burr

Thomas Jefferson ▶

A tie between Thomas Jefferson and Aaron Burr in the election of 1800 led to an amendment that changed how the electors of the Electoral College voted. It made a tie less likely.

Electing the Electors

Starting in 1824, some states began allowing voters to choose the electors. This is how it works today in all states and Washington, DC.

First, before the **general election** in most states, each political party chooses electors for each state. Second, when people vote in the general election, they're really voting for the electors of a political party. For example, if a political party's candidate wins the popular vote, that party's electors are chosen. In most states, the winner receives all the electors available.

Sample presidential ballot, Miami-Dade County, Florida, 2000 ▼

ELECTORS FOR PRESIDENT AND VICE PRESIDENT			COMPROMISARIOS PARA PRESIDENTE Y VICEPRESIDENTE	
Electors for President and Vice President (A vote for the candidates will actually be a vote for their electors.) Vote for One (1) Group	**REPUBLICAN PARTY** GEORGE W. BUSH for President DICK CHENEY for Vice President	4 → ← 4	**PARTIDO REPUBLICANO** GEORGE W. BUSH para Presidente DICK CHENEY para Vicepresidente	Compromisarios para Presidente y Vicepresidente (El voto por los candidatos será en realidad un voto por sus compromisarios.) Vote por un (1) grupo
	DEMOCRATIC PARTY AL GORE for President JOE LIEBERMAN for Vice President	6 → ← 6	**PARTIDO DEMÓCRATA** AL GORE para Presidente JOE LIEBERMAN para Vicepresidente	
	LIBERTARIAN PARTY HARRY BROWNE for President ART OLIVIER for Vice President	8 → ← 8	**PARTIDO LIBERTARIO** HARRY BROWNE para Presidente ART OLIVIER para Vicepresidente	
	GREEN PARTY RALPH NADER for President WINONA LaDUKE for Vice President	10 → ← 10	**PARTIDO VERDE** RALPH NADER para Presidente WINONA LaDUKE para Vicepresidente	
	SOCIALIST WORKERS PARTY JAMES HARRIS for President MARGARET TROWE for Vice President	12 → ← 12	**PARTIDO DE TRABAJADORES SOCIALISTAS** JAMES HARRIS para Presidente MARGARET TROWE para Vicepresidente	
	NATURAL LAW PARTY JOHN HAGELIN for President NAT GOLDHABER for Vice President	14 → ← 14	**PARTIDO DE LEY NATURAL** JOHN HAGELIN para Presidente NAT GOLDHABER para Vicepresidente	
	REFORM PARTY PAT BUCHANAN for President EZOLA FOSTER for Vice President	16 → ← 16	**PARTIDO DE LA REFORMA** PAT BUCHANAN para Presidente EZOLA FOSTER para Vicepresidente	
	SOCIALIST PARTY DAVID McREYNOLDS for President MARY CAL HOLLIS for Vice President	18 → ← 18	**PARTIDO SOCIALISTA** DAVID McREYNOLDS para Presidente MARY CAL HOLLIS para Vicepresidente	
	CONSTITUTION PARTY HOWARD PHILLIPS for President J. CURTIS FRAZIER for Vice President	20 → ← 20	**PARTIDO DE LA CONSTITUCIÓN** HOWARD PHILLIPS para Presidente J. CURTIS FRAZIER para Vicepresidente	
	WORKERS WORLD PARTY MONICA MOOREHEAD GLORIA LA RIV...		**PARTIDO MUNDO DE LOS TRABAJADORES** MONICA MOOREHEAD para Presidente	

In Maine and Nebraska, two electors are given to the winner of the states' popular votes. Then, the winner of the popular vote in each congressional **district** wins an elector too.

Maine

Nebraska

Casting and Counting the Votes

After the general election, each state governor makes an official list of the electors who were chosen by the voters. These electors meet on the first Monday after the second Wednesday in December. Most often, they cast their votes together in their own state capitols.

The electors' votes for president and vice president are recorded on documents, or official papers, called **Certificates** of Vote. These certificates are signed and sent to Washington, DC. They're then counted in the House of Representatives, usually on January 6.

Government Guides

Alexander Hamilton believed electors would be less likely to be corrupt, or dishonest, because they're only appointed for a short time.

As president of the Senate, the vice president reads aloud each state's electoral votes. The vice president also announces the winners of the election.

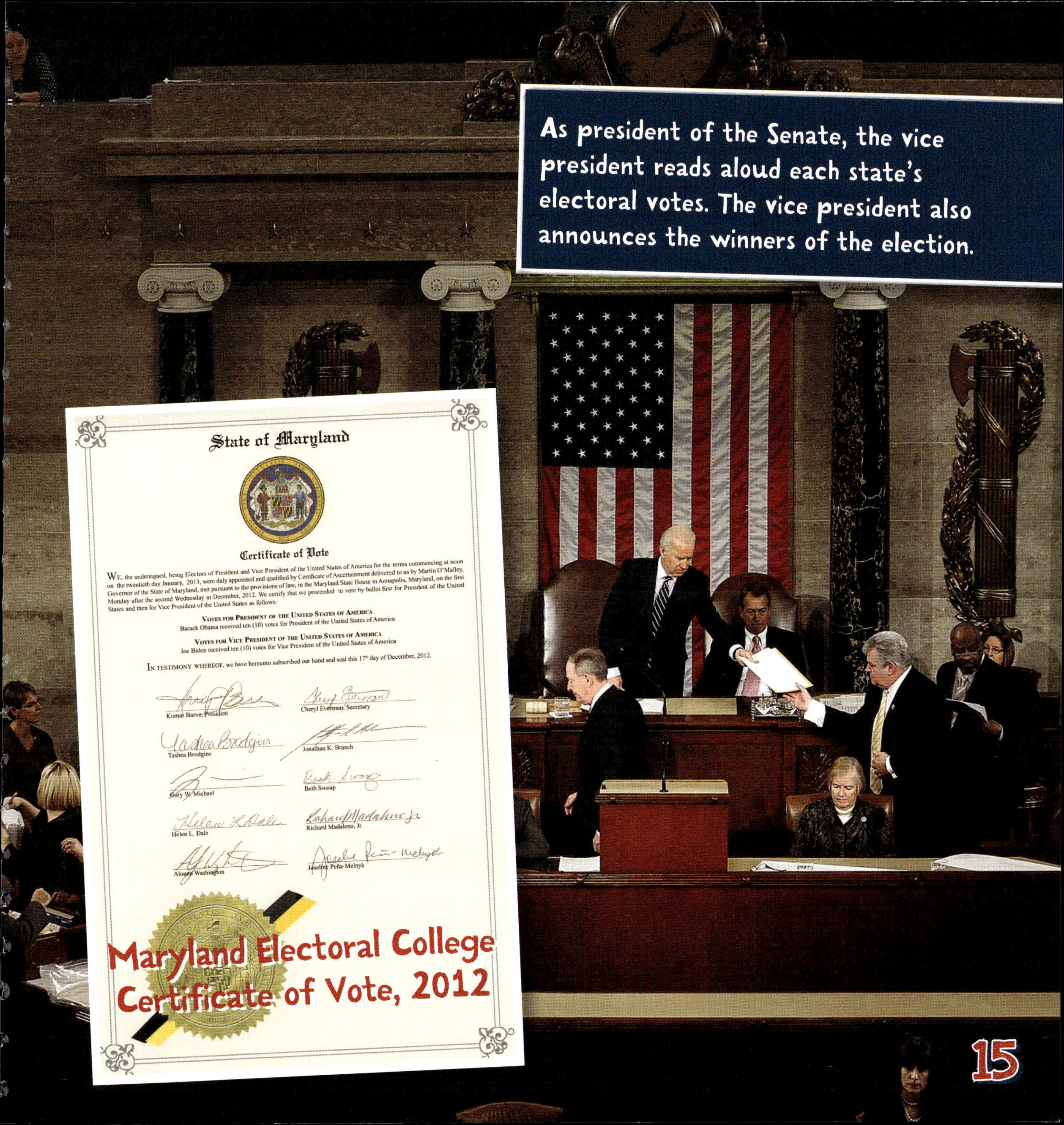

Maryland Electoral College Certificate of Vote, 2012

How They Vote

An elector's vote is expected to agree with the state's popular vote. States may ask electors to make an oath, or promise, to vote this way. No federal law says they have to vote like this. However, some states fine those who don't. Electors who don't vote according to the popular vote are called faithless electors.

There haven't been many faithless electors in U.S. history. Faithless electors have never changed the expected result of an election.

Government Guides

In 2020, the U.S. Supreme Court, the highest court, decided that states can punish faithless electors. Justice Elena Kagan wrote that the Constitution gives states "power over electors" and "electors themselves no rights."

This elector in Colorado was replaced after he decided not to vote for the candidate who won his state's popular vote in the election of 2016.

Justice Elena Kagan

Popular Vote vs. Electoral Vote

The winner of the popular vote isn't always elected president. For example, in the election of 2016, Donald Trump won the presidency even though he lost the popular vote. He received 304 electoral votes, while Hillary Clinton received 227 votes. However, Clinton received almost 3 million more popular votes than Donald Trump.

How'd this happen? Clinton won the popular vote in several big states by a higher number of votes. However, Trump narrowly won popular votes in enough other big states to gain more electoral votes.

Government Guides

In 2004, Al Gore said of winning the popular vote and losing the Electoral College vote in 2000, "You win some, you lose some. And then there's that little-known third category [option]."

Electoral College Results in the 2016 Election

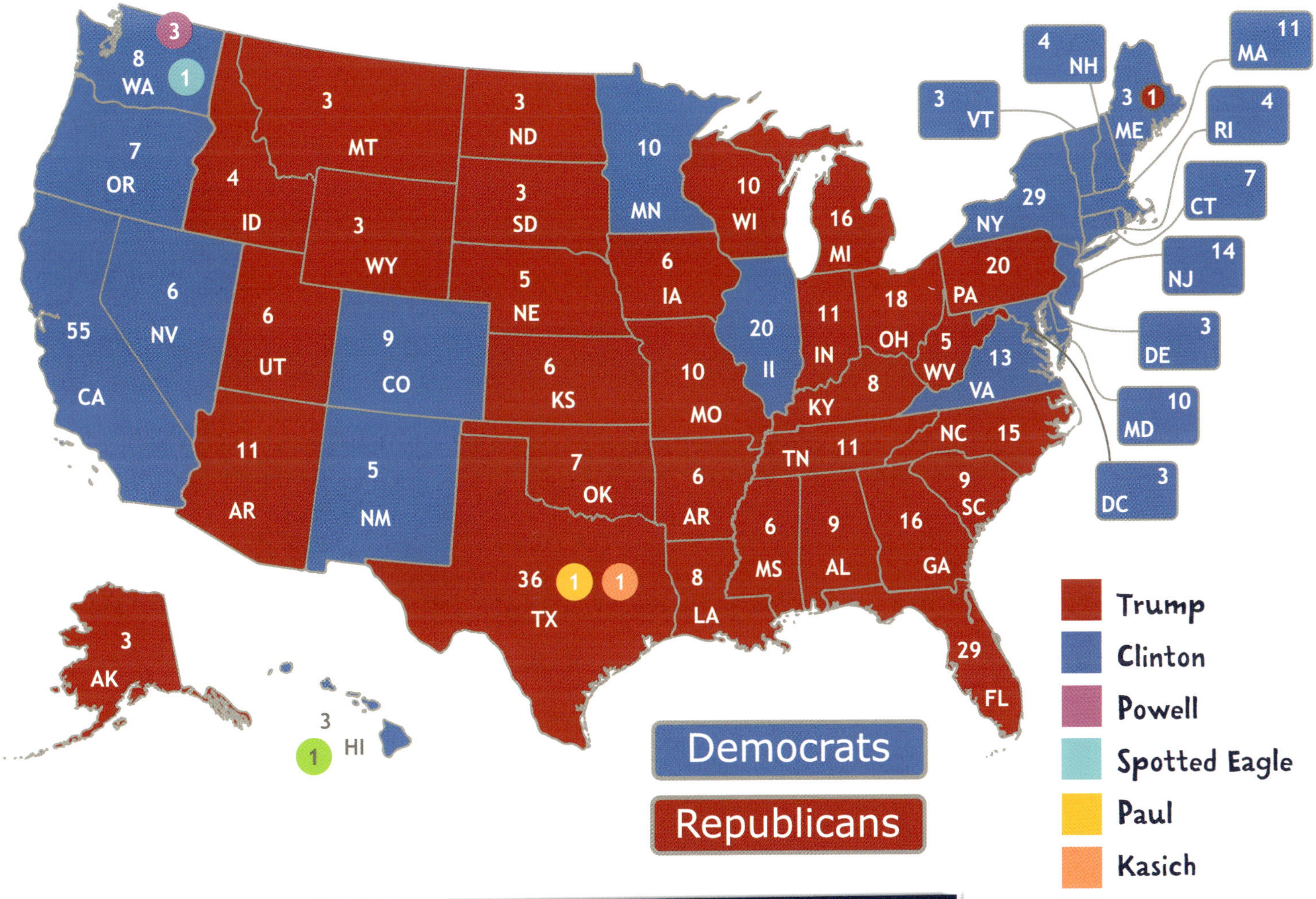

This map shows the electoral vote results of the 2016 presidential election. Note that some electors voted for candidates other than the two main people running.

The Future of the Electoral College

Five times in U.S. history, a candidate has been elected president even though they lost the popular vote. This causes many Americans to question the fairness of the Electoral College. Some say the electoral vote helps smaller states to have power. Others say it makes the popular vote mean less in many states.

Because the Electoral College is a part of the Constitution, it would take a constitutional amendment to change it. This process would require the support of many states. Will it ever happen?

Think About It!

What are your thoughts about the Electoral College? How can we improve our presidential election process?

The Electoral College was set up in the late 1700s. Is it still the best way to pick the U.S. president? Many people have opinions about that!

Glossary

amendment: a change or addition to a constitution

candidate: a person trying to be elected to a position

certificate: a document that gives proof of something

democracy: a government in which every person has the free and equal right to participate

district: an area created by a government for official government purposes

general election: an election involving voters and candidates throughout a country

legislature: a lawmaking body

majority: a number greater than half of a total

political party: a group of people with similar beliefs and ideas about government who work to have their members elected to government positions

popular vote: the choice expressed through the votes cast by eligible voters as opposed to the Electoral College

process: a series of steps or actions taken to complete something

representative: a member of the lawmaking body called the House of Representatives who acts for voters in their district

For More Information

Books

Corso, Phil. *The Electoral College.* New York, NY: PowerKids Press, 2020.

Edwards, Sue Bradford. *The Electoral College.* New York, NY: AV2 by Weigl, 2020.

Meister, Cari. *The Electoral College: A Kid's Guide.* North Mankato, MN: Capstone Press, 2020.

Websites

Elections for Kids
www.gallopade.com/client/electionsForKids/index.html
Learn all about U.S. elections—including more about the Electoral College—at this cool site.

Electoral College
www.ducksters.com/history/us_government/electoral_college.php
Read about some of the pros and cons of the Electoral College here!

United States Presidential Elections
kids.britannica.com/students/article/United-States-presidential-elections/630966
Keep exploring the U.S. presidential election process at this site for kids.

Publisher's note to educators and parents: Our editors have carefully reviewed these websites to ensure that they are suitable for students. Many websites change frequently, however, and we cannot guarantee that a site's future contents will continue to meet our high standards of quality and educational value. Be advised that students should be closely supervised whenever they access the internet.

Index

Biden, Joe 5
Burr, Aaron 10
capitol 14
citizen 6
Clinton, Hillary 18
Congress 6, 8
Constitution 6, 7, 8, 16, 20
election of 1800 11
election of 2016 17, 18
election of 2020 5, 9
faithless elector 16
Founding Father 6
Gore, Al 18
governors 14
Hamilton, Alexander 6, 14
Harris, Kamala 5
House of Representatives 14

Jefferson, Thomas 11
Kagan, Elena 16
Maine 13
Nebraska 13
president 4, 5, 6, 10, 14, 18, 20, 21
Senate 14
Trump, Donald 18
vice president 4, 5, 6, 10, 14, 15
voters 4, 12, 14
Washington, DC 8, 12, 14